Mathew Brady Records

THE CIVIL WAR

by Kari Cornell

Content Consultant

J. Matthew Gallman
Professor of History
University of Florida

DEFINING
IMAGES

Essential Library

An Imprint of Abdo Publishing | abdopublishing.com

abdopublishing.com

Published by Abdo Publishing, a division of ABDO, PO Box 398166, Minneapolis, Minnesota 55439. Copyright © 2018 by Abdo Consulting Group, Inc. International copyrights reserved in all countries. No part of this book may be reproduced in any form without written permission from the publisher. Essential Library™ is a trademark and logo of Abdo Publishing.

Printed in the United States of America, North Mankato, Minnesota
032017
092017

Cover Photo: Mathew Brady/Library of Congress
Interior Photos: Alexander Gardner/Library of Congress, 4, 12–13; 48, 70, 100 (top right); Alfred R. Waud/Harper's Weekly/Library of Congress, 8–9; National Park Service, 10, 40–41; Library of Congress, 15, 31, 32–33, 51, 57, 58, 72–73, 79, 84, 94–95, 100 (bottom right); Brand X Pictures/Stockbyte/Thinkstock, 14–15; Brady-Handy Photograph Collection/Library of Congress, 16; GraphicaArtis/Getty Images, 18–19; The Robin G. Stanford Collection/Library of Congress, 23; Bettmann/Getty Images, 24–25; National Archives and Records Administration, 27; Mathew Brady/Mathew Brady Photographs of Civil War-Era Personalities and Scenes/National Archives and Records Administration, 28, 38–39, 42–43, 52, 74, 83, 88–89, 98–99; Brady's National Photographic Portrait Galleries/Library of Congress, 35, 44, 55, 67, 100 (bottom middle); James F. Gibson/Library of Congress, 36; Alexander Gardner/National Park Service, 46–47, 90–91; Timothy H. O'Sullivan/Library of Congress, 49, 77, 80–81, 100 (bottom left); Nicholas H. Shepher/Library of Congress, 60 ; Alexander Hesler/Library of Congress, 63; Mathew B. Brady/Library of Congress, 64, 100 (top left); Digital image courtesy of the Getty's Open Content Program, 68; Library of Congress/Corbis/VCG/Getty Images, 86; James W. Rosenthal/Library of Congress, 97

Editor: Arnold Ringstad
Series Designer: Becky Daum

Publisher's Cataloging-in-Publication Data

Names: Cornell, Kari, author.
Title: Mathew Brady records the Civil War / by Kari Cornell.
Description: Minneapolis, MN : Abdo Publishing, 2018. | Series: Defining images |
    Includes bibliographical references and index.
Identifiers: LCCN 2016962116 | ISBN 9781532110160 (lib. bdg.) |
    ISBN 9781680788013 (ebook)
Subjects: LCSH: United States--History--Civil War, 1861-1865--Juvenile
    literature. | Brady, Mathew B.,--approximately 1823-1896--Juvenile literature.
    | Photographers--United States--Juvenile literature.
Classification: DDC 973.7--dc23
LC record available at http://lccn.loc.gov/2016962116

CONTENTS

CHAPTER ONE

The Dead of Antietam Shocks the Nation

The Battle of Antietam was the deadliest single-day clash of the Civil War.

Standing side by side in stunned silence, mothers, newspaper reporters, politicians, and tourists alike hunched over to catch their first glimpses of the reality of war. It was October 1862, and the American Civil War (1861–1865) had been raging for a year. The states of the Confederacy, or the South, had seceded from the United States. The Union, or the North, was trying to put down the rebellion and reunite the nation. Here, in the second-floor studio of photographer Mathew Brady's Broadway gallery in New York City, photos from the front lines were on public display for the very first time.

The exhibit, which was called *The Dead of Antietam*, featured photos taken by Alexander Gardner and James Gibson, two photographers who worked for Brady. These photos were like nothing Americans had ever seen. Right there, in stark black and white, were dead soldiers, their lifeless bodies splayed across the misty battlefields near Maryland's Antietam Creek.

One month earlier, on September 17, 1862, Union troops had defeated Confederate forces at Antietam. In 12 hours of combat, approximately 23,000 Union and Confederate troops were killed

GIVING CREDIT WHERE CREDIT IS DUE

The photos that appeared in *The Dead of Antietam* were originally credited to Mathew Brady, not Alexander Gardner, the photographer who was actually capturing the images in the field. This practice of crediting the studio for all images taken by its photographers was common at the time. In early photo studios, many hands were involved in the process of photo production. There were the photographers behind the cameras, the assistants who posed the subjects, the workers who made the prints, and the artists who colored the images by hand. A general credit to the studio often made sense. But once photographers were on the battlefields, taking and developing photos on their own—and sometimes risking their lives in the process—they began to demand individual credit for their hard work. Eventually, Brady began acknowledging the individual photographers along with his studio name.

or injured.[1] In the days that followed, Gardner and Gibson made their way across the battlefield, taking photos of the fallen soldiers. Although the Union had suffered great losses at Antietam, its victory over Confederate troops was significant. The Confederate troops retreated, halting their invasion of the North. Following the Northern victory, President Abraham Lincoln had the successful event he believed he needed to accompany his Emancipation Proclamation. This document declared that all slaves owned by slaveholders living in the Confederate states would be considered free as of January 1, 1863. Antietam would prove to be a key battle in the war. And for the first time, photography would bring a critical battle's aftermath into the view of the public on the home front.

A Shocking Look at the War

Before *The Dead of Antietam*, the American public had visually experienced the war only through the eyes of artists who drew or painted the dramatic battle scenes printed in newspapers. With the advent of a primitive form of photography called the daguerreotype in the United States in 1839, followed by further advances in early photo technology, the camera had become an exciting new way to document people and events. The photographs on display in Brady's

Battlefield sketches were unable to convey the realism provided by Brady's photographs.

gallery that day left a lasting effect on everyone who viewed them. Seeing realistic depictions of fallen soldiers gave people a better sense of war's true horrors.

One *New York Times* reporter summed up the national sentiment about the photos. In an article published in October 1862, the reporter wrote, "Mr. Brady has done something to bring home to us the terrible reality and earnestness of war. If he has not brought bodies and laid them in our door-yards and along the streets, he has done something very like it."[2]

Several photos from the exhibit also appeared in the pages of *Harper's Weekly*, a popular news magazine. Further press coverage about the exhibit, however, did not appear until nine months later, in an article in the *Atlantic Monthly*. There simply was not a demand for such realistic images in the midst of the bloody conflict. In a time when so many people had connections to soldiers on the front lines, it could be heartbreaking to see the faces of the dead on the battlefield. The American people might have preferred to see romanticized paintings of wartime scenes, portraits of generals, or sketches of empty battlefields. Images such as these, which lacked the realism and impact of Brady's photos, were likely more comforting.

Grim images from Antietam show rows of soldiers' bodies lined up for burial.

A Lasting Effect

Despite the lack of press coverage of the Antietam photo exhibit, the photos would have a lasting effect and earn an important place in history. Not only did the Antietam images forever change the way wars would be covered in the press, but they also marked the beginning of what came to be known as photojournalism. In this discipline of reporting, realistic images of newsworthy events are taken as they are happening. When paired with a news story about the event, photos provide a realistic firsthand look at the subject, giving readers the sense of having been there themselves. This style of reporting became the standard practice in the 1900s, when iconic photos became permanently linked to many historical events.

WARTIME PHOTOJOURNALISM

Photojournalism would play an increasingly important role in news reporting during later conflicts. During World War II (1939–1945), for example, the pages of *Life* magazine featured photos of US troops on the front lines in Europe and Asia, including images of actual battles and of soldiers in camp. By this time, motion pictures had been invented, so newsreel footage of troops at the front could be seen in movie theaters as well.

Coverage of the Vietnam War (1954–1975) brought images of war into people's living rooms. During the evening news, Americans gathered around television sets to watch young men at war overseas. The photographers of the Vietnam War era demonstrated the power of photojournalism. As US involvement in the war became more unpopular at home, protesters took to the streets to show their disapproval. These protests and police efforts to control the protesters were also televised. Seeing these disturbing images on a daily basis caused many Americans to push for the government to end the war and bring the soldiers home.

A photo showing Union soldiers standing around a comrade's grave was among many taken by Brady's team at Antietam.

By the time the Civil War finally ended in April 1865, Brady and his team of 20 photographers had taken approximately 10,000 photos of the conflict.[3] Although others were photographing the war as well, it was Brady who was most dedicated to building a photographic historical record of the war and the times. It is largely through Brady's efforts that these photos have been preserved for viewing at the Library of Congress and the National Archives today, more than 150 years after they were taken. And it was through Brady's determination and entrepreneurial spirit that photojournalism emerged as a new medium for documenting historical events as they happen.

Stereograph Views

Many of the photos on display at *The Dead of Antietam* were taken in stereograph format. A stereograph image consists of two photos of the same scene taken at slightly different angles and pasted to a card side-by-side. A viewing device made the image appear three-dimensional. Seeing the photos through a stereograph viewer provided a more intimate viewing experience, particularly at a time when movies and television had not yet been invented. People could examine the look on a soldier's face, or the blood and dust on his clothing. The graphic content and the opportunity to see such depth and detail were shocking to those who came to view the stereograph images in person.

One of the stereograph images from Antietam depicts dead Confederate soldiers in an infamous ditch known as the Sunken Road.

1861 The War For the Union. 1865

1861 Photographic War History. 1865

553.   The "Sunken Road" at Antietam.
[FOR DESCRIPTION OF THIS VIEW SEE THE OTHER SIDE OF THIS CARD.]

NEDERLANDSCHE STEREOSCOOP-MAATSCHAPPIJ
Amsterdam

Stereograph images were placed into simple viewing devices, allowing the observer to experience a simulated three-dimensional effect.

CHAPTER TWO

Mathew Brady's Rise to Fame

Brady himself frequently appeared in photographs, both in his studio and in the field.

Mathew Brady, who would one day become known as the father of American photojournalism, was born to Irish parents near Lake George, New York, in approximately 1823. Little is known about Brady's younger years, other than that he had recurring issues with his eyesight. As a boy, Brady traveled to Saratoga, New York, to receive treatment for eye inflammation. His eyesight was restored, but his vision would never be strong.

An 1838 image created by Louis-Jacques-Mande Daguerre is believed to be the earliest photograph showing a living person, *lower left*.

That trip to Saratoga, however, was Brady's first step on the path to becoming a photographer. There, Brady met William Page, an artist known for painting portraits. Page took Brady under his wing, teaching him to draw. In 1836, Page moved to New York City, where he opened a studio near Washington Square. A few years later, in 1839, 16-year-old Brady moved to Manhattan himself to track down his friend and mentor. In New York City, Page introduced Brady to Samuel F. B. Morse, an inventor and painter best known for inventing a telegraph system in the mid-1830s. Page and Morse had been doing experiments involving daguerreotypes.

THE DAGUERREOTYPE PROCESS

In 1839, Frenchman Louis-Jacques-Mande Daguerre invented the daguerreotype process, a method of capturing an image on a metal plate. Creating a daguerreotype image was complicated. First, a silver coated copper plate had to be polished to a mirror finish. Then that plate was exposed to iodine in a dark box, making the plate sensitive to light. The plate was then transferred to a camera in a lightproof holder. The lens covering of the camera was removed, exposing the plate to light and capturing the image of whatever it was pointing at. Finally, the plate was placed over hot mercury to develop the image, then dipped in a solution of salt to fix the image, making it permanent.

The Daguerreotype Craze

The young Brady was fascinated with the daguerreotype process and attended one of Morse's lectures to learn how to do it himself. He also secured work at A. T. Stewart on Broadway, an early department store. Then, in the early 1840s, Brady opened his own

business. With daguerreotype portraits becoming more popular, Brady saw an opportunity to sell cases to hold the miniature images and protect them from wear. From his shop near Broadway, in a fashionable part of town, Brady began making and selling cases designed to hold small painted portraits and daguerreotypes.

By 1844, Brady had gone into the daguerreotype business himself, opening his own studio at 205 Broadway in New York City. His gallery was strategically located near famed showman P. T. Barnum's American Museum, a popular tourist attraction, and in the same building as Edward Anthony, a supplier of photography equipment. But it was Brady's charm and tenacity that enabled him to rise above the many other daguerreotype artists with studios in the same neighborhood.

A Gallery of Illustrious Americans

Brady immediately set to work, building his reputation as the top daguerreotype artist to visit while in New York. He used his charm to convince famous politicians, celebrities, and wealthy Americans to come sit for a photo in his studio. By the end of his first year in business, Brady had built up a body of work worthy of entering into competitions and fairs. In the fall of 1844, Brady's daguerreotypes won an award at a fair held by the American Institute of the City of New York.

A year later, Brady's daguerreotypes were awarded first prize for best hand coloring and best plain images at the same fair. Around the same time, Brady started collecting images of famous Americans, including one of the last photos taken of an ailing Andrew Jackson. Brady began referring to his gallery as a Hall of Fame, featuring both the photos he had collected and those he had himself taken of various clients. By 1850, the gallery boasted daguerreotypes of several famous Americans of the time, including politicians John C. Calhoun, Henry Clay, and Daniel Webster and author James Fenimore Cooper. A dozen of these photos appeared in Brady's book *A Gallery of Illustrious Americans*, which was published in 1850 and sold for $15 per copy.[1] Meanwhile, Brady continued to win awards for his work. In 1851, he received three gold medals for exceptional daguerreotypes at the Great Exhibition in London, England.

BRADY AND THE PRESS

By the mid 1850s, many newspapers were beginning to use Brady's daguerreotypes as the basis for illustrations that appeared on their pages. The images themselves could not be reproduced using printing technology of the time, so artists instead used daguerreotypes as a reference when creating the woodcuts or engravings that could be translated into print. A Brady image appeared as a woodcut in *Graham's Magazine* in 1854. Brady's images later began to crop up regularly in *Frank Leslie's Illustrated Newspaper* and *Harper's Weekly*.

New Studios

By 1853, Brady had opened a second New York studio. Located in a bigger, more luxurious space at 359 Broadway, this became his main studio. While Brady managed the business at 359 Broadway and oversaw the work of 26 employees, one of Brady's assistants managed the 205 Broadway location.[2]

As word of Brady's reputation as an outstanding daguerreotype artist spread, business boomed. Brady brought on Alexander Gardner as an assistant in 1856. Within two years, Brady opened a third studio in Washington, DC: Brady's National Photographic Art Gallery on Pennsylvania Avenue Northwest. The capital city location made it easier to accomplish a goal

ALEXANDER GARDNER

As Brady's business grew and he continued to struggle with poor eyesight, he hired Alexander Gardner in 1856. Gardner, who had recently emigrated with his family from Scotland, contacted Brady when he arrived in the United States. Gardner was familiar with Brady's award-winning daguerreotypes, which he had seen at the Great Exhibition in London a few years before. Gardner was the perfect addition to Brady's team. Having worked for the *Glasgow Sentinel*, Gardner had experience in journalism, as well as in business and photography. Gardner immediately set to work putting Brady's business affairs in order, insisting that he hire a bookkeeper to manage the company's finances.

In addition to offering business advice, Gardner was instrumental in helping Brady stay on top of the latest photography trends. It was Gardner who introduced the Imperial enlargements that became such a moneymaking hit at Brady's studio. Gardner was also the one who convinced Brady to purchase the four-lens camera needed to produce popular carte de visite photos. People exchanged these small photos much like modern trading cards.

A location on Pennsylvania Avenue, near the nerve center of the US government, brought Brady closer to the important figures he wanted to photograph.

Brady had been talking about throughout his career as a photographer. "From the first," said Brady in an 1891 interview with the New York *World*, "I regarded myself as under obligation to my country to preserve the faces of its historic men and mothers."[3]

Brady put Gardner in charge of managing the Washington, DC, location. But Brady himself spent a great deal of time in the city, coaxing politicians and dignitaries from the nearby hotels on Pennsylvania Avenue into his studio to sit for a portrait.

Advances in Photography

In Brady's studios, his photographers and assistants were expected to keep up with the latest technology to stay ahead of the competition. To this end, Brady's teams began to use the wet-plate process when it became available in 1855, enabling them to improve image quality and speed up the photography process.

WET-PLATE PHOTOGRAPHY PROCESS

Wet-plate photography involved coating a glass plate with a sticky substance called collodion. Collodion allowed a negative impression of the image to stick to the plate when exposed to light. Whereas the old daguerreotype process resulted in a single, one-of-a-kind image on a tin plate that could not be reproduced, having a plate glass negative allowed photographers to print multiple copies of an image on paper.

24

On October 17, 1857, *Harper's Weekly* credited Brady with developing the process of making photo enlargements from an ambrotype, an underexposed photo negative on glass backed by black paper. These enlargements, actually produced by Gardner, were called Imperial prints. Some measured as large as five feet (1.5 m) by seven feet (2.1 m), and their quality was top-notch. In an article published in *Photographic and Fine Art Journal*, one reviewer noted, "His Imperial pictures are certainly the best. . . . He exhibits a group of three full-length life-size on paper . . . as remarkable for its excellence in color, tone and detail, as it is in size."[4]

By 1860, Brady opened the National Portrait Gallery at 785 Broadway in New York City. At this point, Brady was a highly sought-after portrait photographer who had a reputation of being the best in the business. With a thriving business and plenty of money, Brady was in the perfect position to take on a monumental job when the Civil War erupted in April 1861.

BRADY CAPTURES HISTORY

As tensions over the issue of slavery began to build between the North and South in the 1840s and 1850s, Brady was on a mission to photograph as many statesmen as possible. By 1850, he had photographed John C. Calhoun, Henry Clay, Millard Fillmore, Zachary Taylor, Daniel Webster, and many more. Brady identified all of these men as "presidential," meaning they were in a position of possibly running for president at some point in the future.[5] These portraits appeared in the *Gallery of Illustrious Americans* and were also displayed in Brady's studio. By 1859, Brady had photographed every US senator who served in that fateful year, shortly before the Southern states began to secede from the Union. This composite image of the US Senate was created by Brady's studio. By the time the Civil War broke out in April 1861, Brady's studio would be one of the few places where a person could view images of statesmen from both sides of the conflict hanging side by side in the same room.

Brady's composite image was made up of images his photographers had taken over the previous decade.

CHAPTER THREE

On a Mission to Capture History

The ruins captured on film after the First Battle of Bull Run were among the first photographic records of a long, destructive war.

On April 12, 1861, Confederate forces launched an artillery attack on Fort Sumter, a Union fort on a small island off the coast of Charleston, South Carolina, igniting the Civil War. In the days after the event, Brady began to hatch a plan. As a photographer with a well-established reputation for preserving the nation's history in images, the Civil War presented Brady with a new challenge. As Brady would describe years later, he felt compelled to accept it. "I felt that I had to go," Brady said. "A spirit in my feet said 'Go,' and I went."[1]

Brady visited Union officer Major Irvin McDowell to ask permission to follow the Northern army into battle to photograph the war. Although permission was granted, Brady was told he would need to pay his own expenses. Brady agreed to do so.

The Battle of Bull Run

On July 21, 1861, Brady traveled toward the battlefield near Bull Run, a creek in Virginia near the city of Manassas. The fighting there would be known in the Union as the Battle of Bull Run and in the Confederacy as the Battle of Manassas. Accompanying McDowell's troops, Brady wore a straw hat and a long, white linen coat, and carried a large wooden box on his back. He was with 25 to 30 other members of the media, including his assistant Ned House, newspaper reporter Dick McCormick, and *Harper's Weekly* sketch artist Alfred Waud.[2]

Few, including Brady, knew what to expect in battle. Northerners fully believed the Union would win the Battle of Bull Run, extinguishing the Southern rebellion and putting a quick end to the war. A few Northern civilians even packed picnic baskets and traveled to the Virginia countryside to watch the battle unfold.

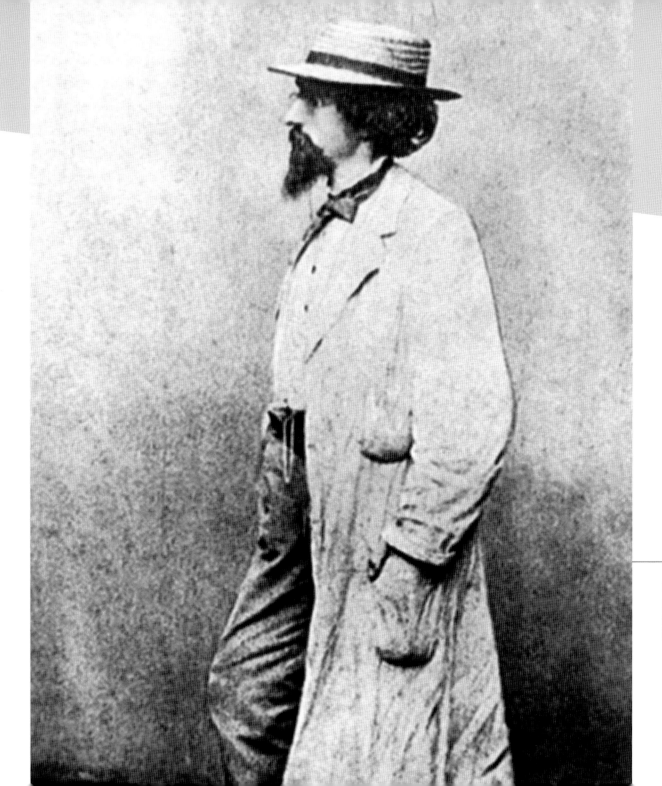

Brady appears in a photograph taken the day after the battle.

Brady's Photo Wagons

When Brady headed out to photograph the Battle of Bull Run, he loaded the photography equipment and chemicals needed to develop photos into a covered wagon. At a time when photos had to be developed in a darkroom immediately after the glass plate was exposed to light, photo wagons were essentially traveling darkrooms. To make the interior of the wagon as dark as possible, photographers wrapped the outside with thick canvas.

Before setting up a photo, photographers huddled in the wagons to mix a batch of collodion, which included the chemicals ethyl ether and acetic or sulfuric acid. After applying the collodion to the glass plate, the photographer dipped the plate into silver nitrate and slid it into a light-safe sleeve before transferring it to the camera. Once the plate had been exposed, the photographer removed the light-safe sleeve and went back to the wagon to develop the image. This involved dipping the glass plate in yet another chemical, pyrogallic

Photography wagons brought sensitive equipment and a small, dark space into the field.

acid. The photographer then rinsed the plate in water, allowed it to dry, and then brushed it with a

coat of varnish to preserve the image. The glass plates were transported back to the photographer's

studio by wagon.

But the Battle of Bull Run was only the beginning of a long war to come. The South was able to hold its own and eventually forced the Union troops to retreat to Washington, DC. Although Brady attempted to take photos of the battle, he returned to Washington, DC, the next day with two damaged photo wagons, which had been flipped during battle, and nothing to show for his efforts. William A. Croffut, a reporter for the *New York Tribune*, wrote about seeing Brady during the Battle of Bull Run:

> *His name was Brady, he added, and the protuberance on his back was a camera. . . . I saw him afterwards dodging shells on the battlefield. He was in motion, but his machine did not seem effective, and when about two o'clock a runaway team of horses came dashing wildly past us, dragging a gun carriage bottom side up, I saw Brady again and shouted, 'Now's your time!' But I failed to stir him. I have often wondered how many pictures he took that day and whether he got out of the battle on our side or the other.*[3]

Although Brady didn't capture any photos at Bull Run, he had made history that day by becoming the first photographer to attempt to take photos while under fire.

Though they could not take action shots, some photographers were able to capture scenes of soldiers and equipment before the battle.

Brady's photographer James Gibson took many shots of US Navy vessels and sailors.

A New Approach

Brady's first attempt to photograph a battle as it was happening had ended in disappointment, and he was in no hurry to put himself back in harm's way. Yet he did not give up. Instead, Brady returned to his studio in Washington, DC, and came up with a new plan.

Brady hired a team of photographers to shoot photos on Civil War battlefields and in army encampments. The team included Gardner, Gibson, Timothy H. O'Sullivan, and George Barnard. Each photographer would come to make a name for himself during the war.

Making History

Brady himself would continue taking photos, but he would focus on studio portraits of esteemed generals, posed photos of regiments in the field, candid shots of camp life, and serene scenes of battlefields long after the fighting had ended and bodies were removed. For the most part, Brady would leave the job of photographing battle scenes to Gardner, O'Sullivan, and the others. When he was not taking portraits, Brady spent his time managing his photo studios, directing photo sittings, and overseeing the work of his photography team.

THE CHALLENGE OF THE ACTION SHOT

As Brady's experience attempting to photograph the Battle of Bull Run shows, taking a photo during the time of the Civil War was not nearly as easy as it is today. Instead of simply pushing a button, photographers had to follow a precise set of steps to successfully capture an image. They had to prepare the glass plate with chemicals, tuck it away in a light-safe sleeve, slide the sleeve into the camera, and finally remove the lens cover from the camera to expose the image. The time of exposure could last minutes. Movement during this exposure period would result in a blurry image. Adding to the challenge was the fact that the images were developed in cramped conditions within the photo wagon. Capturing an image in the 1860s also required a decent amount of light, which was not possible through the hazy smoke of cannon and gunfire on the battlefield. This is why there are no known action shots of Civil War combat.

Generals were among the many subjects of Brady's studio photography.

Brady also remained committed to the task of collecting any war-related photos, including those by other photographers. His ultimate goal was to create a national archive of events and people who shaped the history of the Civil War era. But as Brady and his team of photographers were about to discover, recording the history of this protracted and gruesome war would not be easy.

"BRADY" IS THE MARK OF QUALITY

For some, Brady's name on an image made it more reliable than photos from other sources. With photographers from the North and from the South taking images that portrayed their side in a more positive light, viewers were left to form their own opinions about which sources to trust. Through Brady's own efforts to market the name of his studio, he was able to harness his reputation for quality and win over the trust and loyalty of the public.

One reporter for *Humphrey's Journal*, a publication on photography, claimed to trust only Brady images: "The correspondents of the rebel newspapers are sheer falsifiers, the correspondents of the Northern journals are not to be depended upon, and the correspondents of the English press are altogether worse than either; but Brady never misrepresents."[4]

CHAPTER FOUR

In the Field

Photographers captured grisly post-battle scenes, but their images could not convey what must have been the equally gruesome sounds and smells of the battlefield.

Photography during the 1800s was not a glamorous profession. Brady, Gardner, O'Sullivan, Gibson, Barnard, and the other photographers of the era endured extremely uncomfortable conditions each day they spent photographing battlefields. The tedious and time-consuming process of creating a photo did not translate easily to the world outside the studio. Photographers in the field would spend hours each day crouched down in small, stifling wooden wagons as they mixed chemicals and washed glass plates in processing solutions. The chemicals needed to process photographs emitted toxic fumes that quickly became overwhelming in such a cramped, unventilated space, so photographers had to take frequent breaks for fresh air.

Many variables were completely out of a photographer's control. The slightest unexpected mishap could ruin a photo in an instant. Flies, attracted to the sticky collodion solution used to coat the glass plates, would often land on the finished negative, rendering it unusable. A slight wind was all it took to shift the collodion on the plate, affecting the quality of the image. A drop of sweat rolling off the photographer's forehead could easily land on the image and distort it.

Despite these difficulties, thousands of photos were taken of the war by many photographers. Different styles of Civil War photography emerged during the four-year conflict.

The War through Brady's Lens

Although Brady continued traveling to battlefields after his experience at the Battle of

PHOTOS FROM THE BATTLE OF BULL RUN

In the days that followed the Battle of Bull Run, Brady sent Barnard and Gibson, two photographers from his Washington, DC, studio, to photograph the ruins at the village of Manassas. The village had been devastated during the recent battle. The two returned with approximately 60 images of destroyed bridges, houses with only chimneys left standing, fortifications around Centreville, and the empty battlefield.[1] At last Brady's studio had images from the scene of the battle to send to newspapers and magazines.

42

Portraits often emphasized the subject's heroism and patriotism.

Bull Run, he never again would set foot on one during active battle. The chaos in the final hour at Bull Run had made an impression on him.

Brady's wartime photos showcased his distinctive style. Similar to artists from past conflicts and wars, who embellished battle scenes on canvases, Brady preferred to portray the war in a patriotic, glorious light. Always an entrepreneur, Brady was also trying to capture images that would be popular and profitable.

At heart, Brady was a portrait photographer, and that did not change during the war. Approximately 75 percent of Brady's wartime images are portraits.[2] The rest are largely photos of ships or empty battlefields. Brady was drawn to images of individual soldiers, and he liked to photograph them in camp doing everyday things. Brady took countless portraits of troops with their units. Often, he had them pose for portraits in the natural setting of the encampment. Rather than lean against a chair, as he might have suggested in the studio, Brady had his subjects lean against trees or tent posts. Such poses allowed the subjects to remain still more easily. These photos, although staged similarly to studio shots, had a more realistic look to them. Each photo was made unique by the time of day it was taken, the level of sunlight present, and the location of the soldiers' camp. Those who saw the images could feel as though they were right there with the frontline troops.

Brady battlefield photos were taken only after fallen soldiers had been removed. The serene, countryside images provided those back home with a sense of the landscapes their soldiers were marching through from day to day.

THE BRADY CAMEO

During the war, Brady developed the quirky habit of inserting himself into the photos he took in the field. In a group of people, he might be standing off to the side of the frame. In a quiet landscape shot, he may be leaning against a fence in the distance, often with his back to the camera. Brady's identifying features were always his brimmed straw hat and his long white coat.

No one knows for certain why he would pose in his own photos, but there are a few theories. One may have been to prove he was in the thick of it. After sending so many photographers out into the field to shoot images for his studio, Brady may have wanted to send the message that he had been there too. A second theory is that putting himself in the image was Brady's version of an artist's signature.

Some images from *The Dead of Antietam* depict the lifeless bodies of individual soldiers killed in combat.

Through these photos, people back home could start to understand the lives of their loved ones on the front lines. Brady's photos, though not accurate depictions of the war's horrors, were a comfort to civilians.

A Different Focal Point

Brady or his photographers went to battlefields at Antietam, Gettysburg, the Wilderness, and Petersburg. The photos taken at Antietam and Gettysburg were the most memorable and haunting. Brady traveled to Gettysburg himself in the days following the battle. In the 36 images he and his photography team took there, Brady appears in at least six of them.[3] The Antietam images, photographed by Gardner and Gibson, were famously displayed in Brady's Broadway gallery in the exhibit *The Dead of Antietam* in October 1862. Through their honest photographs, Gardner and Gibson rejected the idea of tiptoeing around the brutality of war. Both of these men photographed the aftermath of the battle, the fallen soldiers still unburied. The corpses strewn on the battlefield shocked those who came to the exhibit.

Writer Oliver Wendell Holmes discussed the photos in an October 1862 article: "The honest sunshine [camera] gives us . . . some conception of what a repulsive, brutal, sickening,

Sobering views of Antietam's aftermath brought the realities of war home for many who lived far from the front lines.

hideous thing it is, this dashing together of two frantic mobs to which we give the name armies."[4]

Parting of Ways

Before the end of 1862, only a couple of months after *The Dead of Antietam*, Gardner left Brady's studio to start his own photography business. His departure would leave a gaping hole in Brady's team.

When he left, Gardner hired away some of Brady's top photographers, including O'Sullivan and Barnard. Most of these photographers had worked for Gardner in the Washington, DC, studio, so they felt more of a connection and a sense of loyalty to Gardner than to Brady.

COMPOSED IMAGES

Photographers were sometimes known to move soldiers' bodies on the battlefield. One famous example of this is an image taken following the Battle of Gettysburg, called *Home of a Rebel Sharpshooter*. Before shooting the photo, Gardner and O'Sullivan moved the body of a soldier from a field to a nearby stone wall to compose a more artistic shot. Gardner also positioned a rifle against the wall to make it look as though the sharpshooter had left it there in the moments before his death.

A portion of Gardner's caption for the image, published in a book he produced after the war, reads:

The sharpshooter had evidently been wounded in the head by a fragment of shell which had exploded over him, and had laid down upon his blanket to await death. . . . Was he delirious with agony, or did death come slowly to his relief, while memories of home grew dearer as the field of carnage faded before him? What visions, of loved ones far away, may have hovered above his stony pillow! What familiar voices may he not have heard, like whispers beneath the roar of battle, as his eyes grew heavy in their long, last sleep![5]

The exact identity of the Confederate soldier pictured in *Home of a Rebel Sharpshooter* is unknown.

49

Gardner also took all of the negatives from 1862, approximately 400 negatives in all.[6] Brady had already made his own copies of many of them, and some appeared in one of his carte de visite catalogs in November 1862.

After Gardner's departure, Brady's studio shied away from publishing graphic photos of the dead on the battlefield. This style, although groundbreaking, was not one Brady wanted to embrace. Brady hired new photographers, including E. T. Whitney and Silas Holmes. And he continued doing what he did best: studio photography.

WORKING FOR THE GOVERNMENT

Photographers were commonly hired by the military to take photos for intelligence gathering. They took photos of enemy supply wagons, weapons, and artillery. Photographers also took images of landscapes to help mapmakers. While employed by Brady, in 1861 Gardner began to work for the Army of the Potomac under General George McClellan. For a time, Gardner closed the Washington, DC, studio so that he could travel with the troops. When Lincoln replaced McClellan with other generals, Gardner's work for the army declined. He later worked for Union generals Ambrose Burnside and Joseph Hooker. Later, in the spring of 1864, Brady became General Ulysses S. Grant's official battlefield photographer.

Gardner established his own gallery in Washington, DC.

CHAPTER FIVE

In the Studio

Union officers and enlisted troops alike posed for portraits in the studios of Brady and other wartime photographers.

As soldiers went off to war, it became a common ritual for them to stop at the local portrait studio and sit for a photo before leaving home. In the uncertain times of war, photos of soldiers who had marched off to the front lines were cherished keepsakes that family members could display at home. The images gave them a connection to their loved ones as they hoped for the soldiers' safe return.

Brady's studios worked hard to keep up with the demand for portraits. In Washington, DC, Gardner outfitted the studio with the cameras required to produce cartes de visite that could be reprinted and passed out to friends and acquaintances. These small cards were not only the perfect size for collecting, they were also affordable.

Brady offered the images for sale soon after each sitting in his gallery. And, for a little extra money, clients could have their portrait retouched or hand colored while they waited.

Collectible Cards

As the war progressed, Brady made a name for himself, creating dignified and sometimes gallant photographs of up-and-coming or already esteemed generals. Among the Union regiments, Brady quickly became the favorite photographer to visit for a portrait sitting. Before long, the walls of Brady's gallery had become a repository of top Union generals, all displayed in life-size Imperial prints. Photos of General George B. McClellan, General Ulysses S. Grant, and General William T. Sherman could be viewed in Brady's galleries. Brady maintained a healthy competition with other photographers in New York and Washington, DC. Each photographer did whatever he could to convince famous

THE FIRST UNION DEATH

One of the soldiers Brady photographed was Colonel Elmer Ellsworth. He stopped to sit for a photo in Brady's New York studio before going off to join his regiment, the Eleventh New York Volunteers, in Alexandria, Virginia. Ellsworth, a law student who had studied under Abraham Lincoln in Springfield, Illinois, would become the first Union death of the war, but he would not die on the front. Ellsworth was shot by innkeeper and Confederate sympathizer James Jackson as Ellsworth attempted to remove a Confederate flag displayed at Jackson's Alexandria inn, the Marshall House. When word of Ellsworth's death reached New York, Brady immediately ordered carte de visite prints of Ellsworth's portrait and offered them for sale in his gallery.

generals to sit at his studio first. Years after the war, in an 1891 newspaper article, Brady boasted that Grant sat for a photo in his studio the minute the popular general arrived from the western front.

Never missing an opportunity to capitalize on the popularity of these wartime celebrities, Brady offered these images for sale as cartes de visite as well. Each cost twenty-five cents.[1] The cards became popular collector's items that were traded among the civilian population. The carte de visite craze led to the very first photo albums, which could hold several dozen cards.

Brady produced carte de visite prints of Elmer Ellsworth, one of the war's first casualties.

In the Galleries

Throughout the war, tourists and locals alike visited Brady's galleries to see photos from the front. Long after Brady displayed Gardner's shocking photos from Antietam in the fall of 1862, he continued to showcase many other photos from major battles. At the time of the Civil War, when motion pictures had yet to be invented, the photographs on display in Brady's galleries provided a glimpse of the reality of war.

The most intimate viewing experience available was to lift a stereograph viewer to the eyes and take in a three-dimensional scene from the front. There were soldiers in camp, wounded men in makeshift military hospitals, posed regiments, fortifications, bridge construction, artillery drills, empty battlefields, and bodies

BRADY IN THE STUDIO

Brady was most at home in the studio. He was a master at warmly welcoming clients into his studio and making them feel comfortable and at ease. Brady typically invited clients to browse the work in the gallery while he and his assistants prepared for the portrait sitting. He had a special talent for this kind of work. He would carefully select props that best suited the subject's personality, profession, or accomplishments and arrange them before an elegant and fashionable backdrop. Then Brady would work with the client, arranging him or her within the stream of natural daylight from a wall of glass windows to perfectly light the subject's face. Photographers often used a vise, a metal frame positioned behind the subject, to keep them completely still when the image was being made. Because of the long exposures required in the early days of photography, one slight movement could blur the image. Brady had a reputation for producing beautifully lit, high-quality studio portraits.

awaiting burial. Collectively, these day-to-day photos told the story of a war that had dragged on for much longer than expected, and of battle-weary soldiers with families anxious to welcome them home.

Washington, DC, Studio Changes Hands

The duration of the war was having an effect on Brady's business. When Brady proposed that he photograph the Civil War and agreed to finance the project himself, he had no idea the conflict would rage for several long years. The cost of sending photographers out into the field with wagons fully stocked with supplies, all while running three studios, had stretched Brady's finances. A few years into the war, Brady claimed to have spent $100,000 of his own money on

As the conflict wore on, supporting crews of photographers in the field became increasingly expensive and hard to sustain.

photographing the war effort.[2] He had a long list of businesses to which he owed money, and they were beginning to demand payment.

So on September 7, 1864, Brady made the decision to sell half of the Washington, DC, studio to James Gibson, a photographer who had worked for Brady since the beginning of the conflict. Gibson had taken over management of the studio after Gardner left, so he was an obvious choice for coownership. The sale freed up some much needed cash for Brady's operations.

CHAPTER SIX

Photographing the President

The earliest known photograph of Lincoln is a daguerreotype produced in 1846 or 1847, when Lincoln was working as a lawyer.

When Abraham Lincoln arrived in New York on February 25, 1860, weary from his cross-country journey by train, he was a lawyer from Springfield, Illinois. Two years earlier, he had lost a bid for the US Senate to Stephen Douglas. From his appearance, it may have seemed unlikely that Lincoln, the surprisingly tall, somewhat awkward, and unpolished man dressed in a rumpled black suit, would one day become the president. But this was exactly what the members of the Young Men's Central Republican Union of New York had in mind.

The group had invited Lincoln to speak to them at Cooper Union, a recently founded college in lower Manhattan, on February 27. Their intentions were clear: to replace William Henry Seward, the current leading Republican candidate for president, with Abraham Lincoln. At the time, Seward was thought to be too extreme in his antislavery views to win the election. Lincoln, like Seward, was against allowing the expansion of slavery into new territories in the west. But Lincoln had a more moderate approach to the topic. Some Republican Party leaders believed Lincoln would be a better candidate to win over more voters.

THE COOPER UNION SPEECH

Lincoln spent more time preparing for the Cooper Union speech than any other speech he made in his political career. His goal was to establish the foundation of his plan for the nation if he were to be elected president of the United States. In the first part of his speech, Lincoln pointed out that 21 of the 39 founding fathers who signed the US Constitution believed the federal government had the legal right to prohibit the expansion of slavery into new territories and states.[1] Then, Lincoln spoke directly to those in the slave states of the South, reassuring them Republicans were not going to abolish slavery where it already existed. And last, Lincoln encouraged Northerners to work tirelessly to ensure slavery did not expand into new territories.

A Visit to Brady's Studio

On the morning of February 27, the day Lincoln was to give his speech at Cooper Union, he arrived at Brady's studio for a photo. A newspaper reporter for the *New York Evening Post*, Richard C. McCormick, described Lincoln's appearance that day:

Photographers took many portraits of Lincoln in the run-up to his presidential campaign.

Along with the Cooper Union speech, Brady's portrait of Lincoln helped introduce the future president to a national audience.

We found him in a suit of black, much wrinkled from its careless packing in a small valise. He received us cordially, apologizing for the awkward and uncomfortable appearance he made in his new suit. . . . His form and manner were indeed odd, and we thought him the most unprepossessing public man we had ever met.[2]

Upstairs in the studio, Brady welcomed Lincoln while the photography assistants set to work, gathering props and preparing for the sitting. In the final photo, Lincoln stands to the left of an architectural column, his left hand resting on a stack of books. Later Brady would explain he had pulled up the collar on Lincoln's shirt and coat to hide his long neck.

Work would continue on the photo after the image was captured. Although the wrinkles in Lincoln's suit remain visible, Brady's assistants used manual techniques to touch up the photo, making lines in his face disappear and "correcting" Lincoln's wandering left eye.[3] All of these slight adjustments gave Lincoln a softer, more pleasing look, which may have helped him appeal to voters.

The Making of an Icon

Lincoln's speech at Cooper Union that evening went off without a hitch, and he was soon invited to give speeches all over New England. Within three months, Lincoln had become the Republican nominee for president of the United States.

Soon after the Cooper Union speech, Lincoln began receiving requests from the press for a photograph, and he directed them to Brady. Soon Brady's image was appearing everywhere. The May 26, 1860, issue of *Harper's Weekly* featured Brady's Cooper Union shot on its cover. Countless other newspapers and magazines used the image as a basis for political cartoons and other illustrations of Lincoln. Printing firm Currier and Ives offered deals on lithographs of the image, and Brady's studio sold many copies of the photo as a carte de visite.

In October 1860, with election day looming, the Cooper Union image appeared in *Frank Leslie's Illustrated Newspaper* with an article about Lincoln and his bid for the presidency. A month later, the newly elected Lincoln lightheartedly credited Brady's Cooper Union photo with playing a part in his successful run for office. "Brady and the Cooper Institute made me President," Lincoln said.[4]

Brady took a photo of Lincoln in a reflective pose in early 1861.

When Gardner took his February 1861 portrait of Lincoln, multiple states had already seceded and the outbreak of the Civil War was only weeks away.

Post-Inauguration Photo Op

The Cooper Union photo session would not be the last time Brady's studio would photograph Lincoln. On February 24, 1861, a few days before his inauguration, Lincoln arrived at Brady's Washington, DC, gallery for a sitting. Brady was out of town, but he left a note with instructions for Gardner to photograph the president-elect.

Although Gardner was a great photographer, studio photographs were not his strength. Artist George Henry Story, who had a studio in the same building as Brady's gallery in Washington, DC, often helped Gardner compose studio photos for important subjects. On this day in February, Gardner went to Story's studio and asked for help posing the president. Story recalled his first glimpse of Lincoln upon entering the studio: "When I went in he was carelessly seated at a table waiting to be posed. He did not utter a word and seemed utterly unconscious of what was going on about him. . . . I did not pose him. It was so characteristic of him, I said, 'Take him as he is.'"[5]

INTO THE LENS

GARDNER PHOTOGRAPHS LINCOLN AT ANTIETAM

This image, one of several taken by Alexander Gardner near Antietam on October 3, 1862, records a tense moment between President Abraham Lincoln and General George B. McClellan, fourth from the president to the left. In the days following the battle at Antietam, Lincoln became frustrated that McClellan failed to attack Confederate troops led by General Robert E. Lee as they retreated. In fact, McClellan had ignored Lincoln's requests to attack for the previous four months. Lincoln decided to pay a personal visit to the general at his encampment to encourage him to pursue the enemy. Lincoln had told his close associates prior to heading out to Antietam, "If General McClellan isn't going to use his army, I'd like to borrow it for a time."[6]

In the end, despite the president's urging, McClellan refused to attack Lee's armies. A month later, Lincoln fired General McClellan, replacing him with Brigadier General Ambrose E. Burnside. Around the same time, photographer Gardner left the employment of Brady, striking out on his own to open a studio in his name.

Lincoln and several of his military commanders met at Antietam two weeks after the battle.

70

A Few Last Photos

On April 19, 1865, Brady or one of the other photographers from his studio took some of the last photos that would be taken of President Lincoln, in a setting no one could have anticipated a week earlier. These photos were of Lincoln's funeral procession. The president had been shot in the back of the head by actor and Confederate sympathizer John Wilkes Booth while attending a performance at the Ford's Theatre in Washington, DC, on April 14. Lincoln died at 7:22 the next morning in a home across the street from the theater.[7]

As the carriage carrying Lincoln's casket made its way down Pennsylvania Avenue from the White House to the US Capitol, mourners lined the street. Lincoln's body would lay in state at the Capitol before being moved to City Hall in New York for viewing. On April 25 in New York,

LINCOLN'S LAST HOURS

On April 15, 1865, artist John B. Bachelder, who had sketched and painted many scenes from the Civil War, proposed the creation of a work to memorialize Lincoln's assassination. Bachelder sketched a scene of Lincoln on his deathbed, surrounded by all the people who visited him in that last evening of his life. Creating the scene from his own imagination, Bachelder presented his idea to Brady, asking him to photograph the people to be featured in the work. Brady agreed, and quickly set to work arranging photo sittings at his Washington, DC, studio. Bachelder gave the photos to Alonzo Chappel, a painter who had worked from Brady's images in the past, to complete the work. By 1868, Chappel had finished two versions of the deathbed scene, but they were never officially accepted and printed for distribution and sale.

Brady captured an image of the funeral carriage transporting the president's casket to the Hudson River Railroad Depot. Behind the funeral carriage marched 11,000 soldiers and 75,000 people, the largest procession in the history of the city to that point.[8]

There, the casket was loaded onto a train car that would depart by rail to Springfield. The funeral car, draped in black banners of mourning, stopped in small towns along the way, following the same route Lincoln took to Washington, DC, after he was elected.

CHAPTER SEVEN

Photography After the War

Stacks of cannonballs remained standing in the ruins of Richmond's destroyed armory.

On the day Lincoln was shot, Brady was nearly 100 miles (160 km) away in the Southern capital of Richmond, Virginia. As many other photographers had done, upon hearing word that the city had fallen to the Union on April 3, 1865, Brady had hastily loaded his equipment into a wagon and headed to Richmond. Many expected that once Richmond fell, the war would be over. Photographers were anxious to photograph parts of the city devastated by the war as a symbol of the South's defeat.

Brady arrived in Richmond on April 12. Besides photographing the ruined city, he had a second mission. Brady was determined to capture images of the defeated General Robert E. Lee.

An Unforgettable Photograph

As the general lingered in Appomattox, Virginia, until April 12, making sure that all of his soldiers had given up their weapons, Brady was contacting Confederate officer Robert Ould and Lee's wife to secure permission to take Lee's photo. It would be a few days before Lee arrived, and Brady would have his work cut out for him arranging a sitting. Lee was known for his dislike of sitting for photographs. But the general was also well aware of his place in history and the value of his photograph to the American people. Lee had met Brady and sat for him before, so there was a trust between the two men. Brady was not afraid to ask for the photograph: "It was supposed that after his defeat it would be preposterous to ask him to sit. I thought that to be the time for the historical picture."[1]

GRANT AT CITY POINT

On his way to Richmond, Brady stopped at City Point, Virginia, which served as General Grant's headquarters during the Petersburg and Richmond Campaigns in 1864 and 1865. General Grant and members of his staff were there, having arrived from Appomattox the previous evening. Brady took several photos of Grant and his staff. He had gotten to know them while serving as Grant's official photographer during the final year of the war. In one of the photos, Brady can be seen posing on the far left of the frame, wearing a stovepipe hat similar to the one Lincoln sometimes wore.

Timothy O'Sullivan captured an image of the site of Lee's surrender in Appomattox.

On April 15, Lee finally arrived in Richmond, riding through town on his faithful horse, Traveller. As Lee approached his home at 707 East Franklin Street, a crowd of people gathered along his route to welcome him home, including the Federal soldiers stationed in Richmond to maintain order.

Brady photographed Lee the next day, Easter Sunday, timing the shot to get the best sunlight. Lee wore his Confederate uniform, but he did not wear a hat or his sword. Lee also wore shoes instead of boots, perhaps signifying a shift from military to civilian life. Brady took photos of Lee posing with Colonel Walter Taylor, his aide, and Major General Custis Lee, his oldest son, who had been taken prisoner by Union troops on April 6. The six photos Brady took on that morning would become famous throughout the North and South, with Brady selling thousands of the images in carte de visite format.

RICHMOND IN RUINS

The photographers flocking to Richmond in the days after the war's end believed the charred and crumbled remains of what had once been a prosperous city would be spellbinding photography subjects. Photos shows soldiers surveying ruined buildings. Many areas of the South were similarly damaged. The vast majority of the war's battles took place in the South. The destruction by Union forces of Confederate infrastructure and supplies reduced Confederate morale and the South's capacity to make war. But some of the damage in Richmond, including the destruction of bridges and useful buildings, was inflicted by Lee's own troops as they fled the falling city.

Lee, *center*, posed on his own front porch for the portrait with his son Custis, *left*, and Walter Taylor, *right*.

Back to the Studio

Many of the photographers who had worked for Brady throughout the war, including Gardner and O'Sullivan, headed to the American frontier to photograph the settling of the West. Brady remained in the East. He returned to the studio to take portraits, in much the same style he had taken before the war. Brady's nephew, Levin Handy, a young, up-and-coming photographer, would eventually share studio space with Brady.

Over the next few decades, Brady continued photographing celebrities, adding poet Walt Whitman and author Mark Twain to his list of notable clients. Brady also maintained

NO PHOTOS AT APPOMATTOX

On April 9, while Brady's competitors were taking countless photos of the ruins of Richmond, Confederate general Robert E. Lee met with Union general Ulysses S. Grant at Appomattox Court House, Virginia. After great losses at Petersburg, Virginia, and following the fall of Richmond, Lee and his Army of North Virginia were cut off from supplies. His soldiers were hungry and lacked critical equipment. The Confederate army had reached the end, and Lee knew it. He had no choice but to negotiate a peaceful surrender. Lee's forces were not the only Confederate troops still in the field, but his was the most formidable force, and its surrender made the war's end inevitable. The remaining pockets of Confederate troops surrendered during the next few months.

The meeting between Lee and Grant was cordial. Both had experienced the same horrible war and knew it was time to reconcile. The Union offered generous terms for surrender. But at this historic moment, no photographers were present to record the handshake between the leaders of the Union and Confederate armies. Illustrations are all that exist to commemorate the meeting that finally put an end to America's bloody Civil War.

his tradition of photographing presidents. Between 1865 and 1877, Andrew Johnson, Ulysses S. Grant, and Rutherford B. Hayes all went to Brady's studio for sittings. In June 1880, Brady photographed James A. Garfield, the last president who would sit in his studio.

Financial Woes

Although Brady continued to work as a photographer after the war, the financial troubles that had started back in 1862, when Gardner had left Brady's studio, grew worse. Brady was a master salesman, art director, and marketer, but he did not have a keen business sense. Gardner had been instrumental in keeping organized business records and insisting that Brady hire a bookkeeper.

To add to Brady's troubles, his decision to sell half of the Washington, DC, studio to Gibson in the fall of 1864 had not been a good one. According to Brady, over the next four years, Gibson took out a mortgage on the Washington, DC, studio, collected the debts he could, and left for Kansas, never to be heard from again. On June 26, 1868, Brady filed a lawsuit against Gibson in an attempt to recoup his losses from the alleged mismanagement. When the Washington, DC, gallery went bankrupt and was sold at public auction for on July 23, 1868, Brady was the

Famed poet Walt Whitman is the subject of a postwar Brady portrait.

Brady fell into hard times late in his life.

only bidder. He purchased his gallery back for $7,600.[2] This is equivalent to more than $120,000 in 2015 dollars.[3] But Brady remained in financial trouble, and in 1873 he was forced to declare bankruptcy. By court order, Brady's negatives and photography equipment were seized by New York State. Through it all, Brady seemed to remain confident that once he sold his collection of Civil War images, he would be debt-free.

CHAPTER EIGHT

Creating a National Archive

Brady's gallery became a photographic museum of the war's people and landscapes.

Throughout his lengthy and storied career, Brady always maintained a strong sense of history. In his work as a photographer, he made it a lifelong goal to collect and capture images of historically significant people, places, and events. He used the walls of his galleries in New York and Washington, DC, to display and showcase those images for all to see. And, when the Civil War erupted in April 1861, Brady knew he had to record the conflict as completely as he could through photographs.

Although the government granted Brady permission to photograph the events of the war, it provided no financial support for his efforts. With a prospering photography business and plenty of money to launch the project, Brady proceeded to hire a team of photographers and acquire the equipment needed to capture the war in images. At that point, Brady had no idea how long the war would go on. He lived in New York, where many believed Union troops would defeat the rebellious South in a year or less.

But this was not the case. Northern armies battled Southern armies for four long, costly years. By the time the war had ended, Brady had spent vast amounts of his own money. According to Brady, the resulting archive of photos was of historical significance and should be made available to the American public for all to see.

The New York Historical Society

In 1866, Brady contacted the New York Historical Society, asking if it would be interested in purchasing his extensive collection of Civil War photography. He called it "Brady's National Historical Collection," and he was asking a lofty price of $30,000.[1] The Historical Society agreed

Brady's collection of images was significant. In fact, from February 1866 through March 1866, his wartime photos were on display in galleries at the society.

The New York Historical Society agreed to buy the collection, but the deal fell through, and no money changed hands. The society had talked of building a new facility in Central Park, where Brady's collection would have its own room. Due to a lack of funding, however, that proposal was canceled. Brady continued searching for a buyer.

Selling the Collection

Brady approached his friends and acquaintances, hoping to gather the support he needed to prove his collection was of historical significance. When it seemed the New York Historical Society was not going to buy the images, Brady asked General Grant and Admiral David Glasgow Farragut to vouch for the value of his collection as a national treasure. Both readily agreed.

Brady also garnered support from the National Academy of Design, an organization consisting of many of his friends. The academy endorsed Brady's collection, referring to it as a

"nucleus of a national historical museum, reliable authority of Art and illustrative of our history."[2] The press even chimed in, offering praise of Brady's images as reliable retellings of the events of the war.

Still, no one stepped forward to purchase the collection. There are a few possible reasons for the lack of interest in Brady's work. For one, the sentiment throughout the country in the years immediately following the war was to try to forget about the conflict and move on. Brady's images only served as a reminder of those divisive, destructive years. Furthermore, many of the images in Brady's collection were already readily available in books, as cartes de visite, and as stereograph cards his studio had sold throughout the war years.

In 1869, perhaps in the hope of bringing more attention to the collection and making some money on the images, Brady published a book, the *National Photographic Collection of War Views and Portraits of Representative Men*. But a buyer for his wartime photo collection did not come forward.

Negatives at Public Auction

Meanwhile, Brady's financial woes continued. In 1874, a warehouse owner in New York had had enough of Brady's unpaid bills. For years, Brady had stored 2,250 negatives from the Civil War in the warehouse.[3] The owner had likely heard about Brady's bankruptcy proceedings the year before and decided to auction off Brady's property. Secretary of War William W. Belknap bid on the negatives and won, paying $2,500 for them.[4]

When Brady learned of the transaction, he was fuming with anger. He confronted Belknap about buying his collection at a price far below what it was worth. Belknap argued his case, stating that his purchase through the auction

MISSING NEGATIVES

In the early 1870s, when Brady was trying to avoid bankruptcy, he handed over many of his Civil War negatives to E. & H. T. Anthony, a photography equipment supplier based in New York. Anthony had extended credit to Brady for years but was now demanding payment. With no money to spare, Brady gave the company several of his negatives in payment for debt, with plans to eventually pay it back and collect the images. However, Brady never returned for the images. A decade later, John C. Taylor, a Civil War veteran and collector, found the images in the attic of an old building owned by Anthony. Taylor purchased the rights to the negatives and made them part of the Ordway/Rand Collection. In 1912, Edward Bailey Eaton used the negatives, which included the work of Brady and other photographers, to publish *The Photographic History of the Civil War*. In 1943, the Library of Congress purchased the Brady negatives. They became part of the Civil War Glass Negatives and Related Prints collection.

was legitimate. At the same time, Belknap offered to help him finally make a deal with the US Congress to purchase the collection.

In 1875, Congress agreed to purchase Brady's collection of approximately 3,467 negatives for $25,000.[5] Although the amount of the sale did not come close to the $100,000 figure Brady claimed he had spent to produce the images, it did cover the cost of his debts. Brady's images formed the foundation of a collection of Civil War negatives stored at the War Department Library. In 1940, the images were passed along to the National Archives, where they remain today.

Leaving Behind a Legacy

After the sale of his collection, Brady worked as a photographer for another 20 years. He shared a studio with his nephew, Levin Handy, and for the most part stuck to portrait photography.

CLOSING THE WASHINGTON, DC, STUDIO

By 1880, Brady was over his head in debt once again. The Washington, DC, studio had become run down, and Brady had fallen behind in the rent. He tried to save the studio by mortgaging most of the photography equipment and artwork within it, including the famous chair that Lincoln and many others had sat in while being photographed, but it was no use. Much of the money he was able to take in through sales of his assets went to his nephew, Levin Handy, who had helped Brady stay afloat during the previous few years. In November 1881, Brady was forced to shutter Brady's National Photographic Art Gallery for good after 24 years in business.

On April 16, 1894, Brady was crossing a street in Washington, DC, when he was hit by a horse-drawn cart and broke his ankle. He would never fully recover from the accident, and he always walked with the help of a crutch. Brady moved back to New York in April 1895, where a handful of old friends cared for him and helped him find a place to live. Less than a year later, on January 15, 1896, Brady died at Presbyterian Hospital of complications from Bright's disease. Only two weeks later, on January 30, he had been scheduled to give a lecture at Carnegie Hall about his life and work.

Brady died nearly penniless. In his quest to curate a collection of images that defined the Civil War era, Brady had risked everything. In Brady's words, "No one will ever know what I went through in securing those negatives. The world can never appreciate it. It changed the whole course of my life."[6]

Although Brady's fame had faded by the time he died, he left behind a lasting legacy. Through the images Brady collected and the

WHERE ARE BRADY'S IMAGES?

Many of Brady's images are part of the Brady-Handy Collection and can be viewed online through the Library of Congress Photographs Online Catalog. The Library of Congress purchased the collection, which includes approximately 10,000 negatives, original prints, and copies from the Civil War, from sisters Alice H. Cox and Mary H. Evans in 1954.[7] Cox and Evans were the daughters of Brady apprentice Levin Handy. Other Brady images can be seen on the website of the National Archives.

Brady is buried in Washington, DC.

Brady's photographs give modern
viewers a window into some of the most
consequential years in US history.

photographs he and his team took, he played a significant role in preserving the story of the

American Civil War in pictures. It is because of Brady, who valued history and felt driven to

capture the events and people of the war in images, that photojournalism came to exist. In

their quest to record history and stay one step ahead of the competition, Brady and other

photographers pushed the limits of photography and the technology of the day, advancing

the medium well beyond what had been possible in the years before the war.

PHOTOGRAPHING THE CIVIL WAR

1. ## Abraham Lincoln, Cooper Union

   Mathew Brady took this photo in his New York studio on February 27, 1860, the day presidential hopeful Abraham Lincoln gave his famous campaign speech at Cooper Union.

2. ## The Dead of Antietam

   The photos of dead soldiers at the Antietam battlefield shocked all who saw them, bringing home the reality of war in black and white.

3. ## Home of the Rebel Sharpshooter

   For this image, the photographers moved the body of a Confederate soldier to compose a more artistic shot against a stone wall.

4. ## Elmer Ellsworth

   Brady photographed Union soldier Elmer Ellsworth before Ellsworth joined his regiment in Alexandria, Virginia. Ellsworth became the first Union death of the war. Brady offered carte de visite of this image for sale in his gallery.

5. ## General Robert E. Lee

   Brady took this photo of General Lee on April 16, 1865, following the Confederate surrender. The six photos Brady took on that morning would become famous throughout the North and South.

Quote

"Mr. Brady has done something to bring home to us the terrible reality and earnestness of war. If he has not brought bodies and laid them in our door-yards and along the streets, he has done something very like it."

—New York Times *reporter, October 1862*

GLOSSARY

bookkeeper
A person who manages financial records.

civilian
A person not serving in the armed forces.

collodion
A sticky substance used on a glass plate to capture a negative image.

daguerreotype
An early photographic process using a silvered plate brushed with iodine, exposed to light, and then developed using mercury vapor.

darkroom
A room in which light is blocked out and photographs are developed.

entrepreneur
A person who organizes and operates a business or businesses.

exposure
The action of allowing light to enter a camera, creating a photograph.

fortification
A structure built to withstand an attack.

lithograph

An image created by a process in which a flat surface is treated to repel ink except where it is required to create the image.

negative

The reverse of an image that appears on a glass plate or film when it is exposed to light.

photojournalism

The art of communicating news through photographs.

regiment

An army unit typically commanded by a colonel.

retouch

To make changes to a photograph, often to improve the subject's appearance.

secede

To formally withdraw from a political union.

tenacity

Perseverance and determination.

unprepossessing

Unattractive or unappealing to the eye.

ADDITIONAL RESOURCES

Selected Bibliography

Rosenheim, Jeff L. *Photography and the American Civil War*. New York: Metropolitan Museum of Art, 2013. Print.

Savas, Theodore P. *Brady's Civil War Journal: Photographing the War 1861–65*. New York: Skyhorse, 2008. Print.

Wilson, Robert. *Mathew Brady: Portraits of a Nation*. New York: Bloomsbury, 2013. Print.

Further Readings

Cummings, Judy Dodge. *Civil War*. Minneapolis, MN: Abdo, 2014. Print.

Gallman, J. Matthew, and Gary W. Gallagher, eds. *Lens of War: Exploring Iconic Photographs of the Civil War*. Athens, GA: U of Georgia P, 2015. Print.

Streissguth, Tom. *The Battle of Antietam*. Minneapolis, MN: Abdo, 2017. Print.

Websites

To learn more about Defining Images, visit **abdobooklinks.com**. These links are routinely monitored and updated to provide the most current information available.

For More Information

For more information on this subject, contact or visit the following organizations:

MANASSAS NATIONAL BATTLEFIELD PARK

12521 Lee Highway
Manassas, VA 20109
703-361-1339 x0
https://www.nps.gov/mana/index.htm

Visit the battlefield where Mathew Brady first attempted to take photos of troops engaged in combat.

NATIONAL PORTRAIT GALLERY

Eighth and F Streets NW
Washington, DC 20001
202-633-8300
http://npg.si.edu

Tour the *American Presidents* gallery on the second floor to see Mathew Brady's portraits of Abraham Lincoln.

SOURCE NOTES

CHAPTER 1. *THE DEAD OF ANTIETAM* SHOCKS THE NATION

1. Vaughn Wallace. "150 Years Later: Picturing the Bloody Battle of Antietam." *Time*. Time, 17 Sept. 2012. Web. 5 May 2016.

2. "Mathew Brady: Photographer." *Civil War Trust*. Civil War Trust, 2014. Web. 11 Apr. 2016.

3. "Mathew Brady." *History Channel*. History Channel, 2009. Web. 11 Apr. 2016.

CHAPTER 2. MATHEW BRADY'S RISE TO FAME

1. Mary Panzer. *Mathew Brady and the Image of History*. Washington, DC: Smithsonian, 1997. Print. xv.

2. Ibid. xviii.

3. Alan Trachtenberg. *Reading American Photographs: Images As History—Mathew Brady to Walker Evans*. New York: Farrar, 1990. Print. 33.

4. Mary Panzer. *Mathew Brady and the Image of History*. Washington, DC: Smithsonian, 1997. Print. xvii.

5. Ibid. 62.

CHAPTER 3. ON A MISSION TO CAPTURE HISTORY

1. Bob Zeller. *The Blue and Gray in Black and White: A History of Civil War Photography.* Westport, CT: Praeger, 2005. Print. 3.

2. Ibid. 53.

3. Ibid. 57.

4. Mary Panzer. *Mathew Brady and the Image of History.* Washington, DC: Smithsonian, 1997. Print. 102.

CHAPTER 4. IN THE FIELD

1. Robert Wilson. *Mathew Brady: Portraits of a Nation.* New York: Bloomsbury, 2013. Print. 148.

2. Mary Panzer. *Mathew Brady and the Image of History.* Washington, DC: Smithsonian, 1997. Print. 103.

3. Robert Wilson. *Mathew Brady: Portraits of a Nation.* New York: Bloomsbury, 2013. Print. 159.

4. Ibid. 139.

5. "The Case of the Moved Body." *Library of Congress.* Library of Congress, n.d. Web. 5 Dec. 2016.

6. Robert Wilson. *Mathew Brady: Portraits of a Nation.* New York: Bloomsbury, 2013. Print. 139.

SOURCE NOTES CONTINUED

CHAPTER 5. IN THE STUDIO

1. Bob Zeller. *The Blue and Gray in Black and White: A History of Civil War Photography.* Westport, CT: Praeger, 2005. Print. 74.

2. Robert Wilson. *Mathew Brady: Portraits of a Nation.* New York: Bloomsbury, 2013. Print. 199.

CHAPTER 6. PHOTOGRAPHING THE PRESIDENT

1. Gary Finke. "The Cooper Union Address: The Making of a Candidate." *Lincoln Home: National Historic Site, Illinois.* National Park Service, n.d. Web. 15 May 2016.

2. Robert Wilson. *Mathew Brady: Portraits of a Nation.* New York: Bloomsbury, 2013. Print. 63.

3. Christopher Benfey. "Theater of War: The Real Story Behind Mathew Brady's Civil War Photographs." *Slate.* Slate, 30 Oct. 1997. Web. 15 May 2016.

4. Robert Wilson. *Mathew Brady: Portraits of a Nation.* New York: Bloomsbury, 2013. Print. 65.

5. Ibid. 67.

6. Jeff Rosenheim. *Photography and the American Civil War.* New York: Metropolitan Museum of Art, 2013. Print. 12.

7. Robert Wilson. *Mathew Brady: Portraits of a Nation.* New York: Bloomsbury, 2013. Print. 195.

8. Ibid. 194.

CHAPTER 7. PHOTOGRAPHY AFTER THE WAR

1. Robert Wilson. *Mathew Brady: Portraits of a Nation*. New York: Bloomsbury, 2013. Print. 191.

2. Mary Panzer. *Mathew Brady and the Image of History*. Washington, DC: Smithsonian, 1997. Print. xxi.

3. "Inflation Calculator." *Westegg*. Westegg.com, n.d. Web. 5 Dec. 2016.

CHAPTER 8. CREATING A NATIONAL ARCHIVE

1. Mary Panzer. *Mathew Brady and the Image of History*. Washington, DC: Smithsonian, 1997. Print. 115.

2. Ibid. 116.

3. Bob Zeller. *The Blue and Gray in Black and White: A History of Civil War Photography*. Westport, CT: Praeger Publishers, 2005. Print. 190.

4. Ibid. 191.

5. Ibid. 190.

6. Ibid.

7. "Brady-Handy Collection." *Library of Congress*. Library of Congress, n.d. Web. 23 May 2016.

INDEX

About the Author

Kari Cornell is a freelance writer and editor who loves to read, garden, cook, run, and make clever things out of nothing. She is the author of *The Nitty Gritty Gardening Book: Fun Projects for All Seasons, Women in the Civil War,* and several cookbooks and biographies for kids. She lives in Minneapolis, Minnesota, with her husband, Brian, two sons, Will and Theo, and her crazy dog, EmmyLou.